THIS NOTEBOOK BELONGS TO ....

CONTACT ....

Day 1

CONS:
- short lesson plans
- vocab too difficult
- not engaging enough topic
- lesson not well understood
- repetitive usage of Spanish
- some disciplinary problems
- <u>begging</u> for participation
- students at <u>very</u> different levels.
- translating

PROS:
- correcting discipline easier than I thought it to be.
- technology worked fine.
- good relationship building with students
- mistakes of mine were so terrible, easy to pin point and avoid <u>forever</u>.
- kids liked making name tags
- all students generally respectful + sweet, + apologetic when I prefer

Día 2 - Preguntar

1. ¿What is a question?
2. examples of questions from T
3. T asks for examples - writes on board
4. Instructions for Rapid fire
5. T models (I do)
6. T asks (you do)
7. Test Round (we do)
8. Class does task
9. Recap/Review vocab from task
10. Introduce ~~●~~ X system for next week.

Xtra activities:
- ~~hangman~~
- hangman ●
- Is ice cream good? (ask students to answer!)

Day 2

PROS:
- more english from kids
- better discipline
- some english communication between kids
- kids more talkative
- more movement

CONS:
- content too difficult
- not enough activities
- topic too broad

Day 3 (floater)

PROS:
- seeing discipline styles of diff teachers + how students respond
- getting practice in of student names while guiding them to classes
- insight on everyone's approach to teaching

CONS: ss getting distracted as I walk in

↳ homeroom interesting because there's no real structure, but I like it b/c gain more insight on ss personalities + knowledge.

Day 4

Up: If you're wearing a (<3 kids) color shirt, stand up. If you're wearing (color) shoes, stand up. If you have long hair, sit down. Good job!

1st task: SS describe toy T brought. Color? Big? Small? T holds toy behind back while SS ask questions about it.

Middle: Powerpoint w/ examples (3)

Main task: 1 student facing board w/ eyes covered. T picks ~~~~ object in classroom. SS have to ~~~~ describe the object T chose to S facing board.

Wind down: How would you describe me to ~~someone~~? My shirt, my hair? my shoes? glasses?

Alt activity: ① ~~~~ no vision rules
② Guess who
③ I Spy

Potential Topics

- Halloween: this is halloween song
- ~~weather~~ Transportation (plane, car, train, horse, bus, skates, hot air balloon, rocketship, (cowboy) boat (board?))
- alt
- Shapes (thursday lesson?)
- everyday life · I spy ← activity
- plants/nature: beach, farm, forest, desert

- loud vs. quiet : ~~~~ activity: video?
  is a dog louder than cat?
  car louder than train?

  The _____ is _____.

maracas
candy   ← homeroom!
pencils

ese = that   Palabras Nuevas   esto = this
esas = those

derrotar	—	defeat / beat
rechazo	—	reject / turn down
trozos	—	pieces
alcanza	—	catch up
*deseo	—	I wish
sitio	—	site
desde	—	from
expresar	—	express
~~volar~~	—	fly
intento	—	try / attempt
dijeron	—	they said
perder	—	lose
pierde	—	he/she lose
crear	—	create
cuaderno	—	notebook
andar	—	walk ?
perteneces	—	you belong
ofrecer	—	offer ?
descansa	—	rest
tira	—	pull / throw
pronto	—	soon
saltar	—	jump
lugar	—	place
campesinas	—	peasants

Rasuradoras — Razors
próxima — Next
lograr — achieve
reglas — rules

Day 4 Reflection

Halloween

PROS: SS were engaged + interested, activity seemed to be fun + helpful w/ remembering/recognizing costume names, introduction of new vocab accidentally (lights, decor), kids liked "trick or treat"

CONS: Some classes were more advanced + whizzed through lesson quickly. Didn't plan enough activities. Struggled thinking on my feet to add new activities vs repetition, lots of use of powerpoint, emotional day for me.

Day 5 Reflection

Why I ♡ my Parents

PROS: Recognizable language for SS, SS able to think creatively.

CONS: Time management, too much writing, discipline was rough

Day 6 Reflection

LOUD VS. QUIET

PROS: SS had a lot of fun screaming + whispering. Short review of nouns from earlier lessons. Some sentence usage w/ comparatives.

CONS: Time management AGAIN, heavily relying on powerpoints, some SS did not like the loud noises of screaming (2 specifically)

Day 7 Reflection

SUPERHEROS/CHARACTERS

PROS: SS very responsive to answering questions about their favorite characters. Running activity went well and SS did really well. Time management got better throughout the day. Best day and lesson plan yet!

CONS: Not enough variance in difficulty for ~~funn~~ weaker students. Got very overwhelmed that 1/4 class didn't get it

hard time explaining instructions

Day 6 LP — July 9, 2019

Warmup: Who are these characters? (ppt)
5 min
☼ "Goodmorning" written on the board. -OR- "Happy Tuesday!"

Vocab: Fast, strong, long hair, magic, nice, short/tall, funny
10 min

Hot Seat Activity: "Spiderman" on board w/ chosen child facing class
~~10~~ 15 20 min
5-10 min → 3 rounds
Maybe 2 SS from 2 teams

Instructions + modelling
5-10 min
I do, we do, you do! →

Teacher Input
5 min, 2 rounds →
Describe S in the room, (hair, clothes, nice, smart, funny, etc.) SS have to guess who it is.

5-10 min, 2 rounds
Have a S describe someone in the room. SS + T have to guess who it is. T write description on the board.

Wind-down/Summary: Categories

Warmup games Ideas

* ✶ categories: superheroes? 2 lines. ✶
  who calls out first.

* basketball. 2 teams. 1 team asks
  "what does he do"

* quick show:
  ↳ slap game flashcards
  ↳ close eyes. what's missing?
     - can pass to other SS
  ↳ pull away flashcards. SS have to
    say vocab before T pulls away.

▷ I do we do you do
   - get strongest SS to help
▷ Race to get flashcard and ~~xxxxx~~
✶ touch the card in under 5 seconds

What is your favorite show?

~~eating dinner w/~~
~~friend. eating flan~~
~~she says a joke +~~
~~laughs~~
~~I choke and she~~

Riding in car.
Music loud. Windows down.
I had my hand out window.
She rolls window up. ~~She~~ I
yell and wiggle and she thought
I was dancing until ~~##~~ she
finally saw my face!

Day 8
Reflection

topic: Day 8 LP   Lang feature...

Warmup:

Beach
Sports
Video Games
Pets
Transportation
emotions
Preopositions
questions

Desserts Day 7

Warmup		different desserts on PPT.	Standard 5
	5	does anyone know?	
	5	categories (get to 5!)	
Pre-task	5-10	Vocab. desserts	
Activity #1	10	Class circle on floor. FC in middle. SS read ea. 1. T turns them all over, mixes "Which one did I take away?" 3-5x depending	
IdK	5	T draws ~~on board~~ PPT "I like" "I love" "I don't like" "I hate" w/ :) ♡ :(😠 Asks SS about diff desserts.	
Activity #2	5-10	T has Like, Love, etc. in 4 corners of room. SS have to decide where to run in 5 secs. + T will ask random for sent.	
Activity #3	5-10	Back in floor circle. T plays music. Hands out a few cards. When music stops, SS have to say I hate, love, etc. the pic on flashcard.	
Tickey OTD		T holds up flashcard w/ word covered. What's this?	
alt activity		fast card	

Assignments due Aug 2nd

1. Reflection essay 2 pages
2. Daily Reflection 1/2 page /ea.
3. Final Lesson plans (8)
4. Scan teaching evals [PDF]
5. John + Hilda supervisor evals.
6. Pedagogical beliefs

L2 Teaching Philosophy
beliefs about L2 teaching

How L2 Learning Occurs: (3rd) Via repetition, relatable concepts, informal teaching (grammar via teacher usage)

Teacher's Role in Classroom: (4th) Motivator, language knower, mindful/educated facilitation, classroom manager

Environment: Open environment, relatable, able to err + ask questions, engaging, comfortable, managed, conversation-driven but not confident/pressurey (topics that interest ss) (2nd topic)

Why? (4½) Practice makes perfect. I've found that interacting w/ new languages whether in class or in RW leads to better recollection of language. Making a CR convo based provides more opps for students to practice speaking + listening skills thus leading to potential ease w/ reading + writing skills

What should SS learn?	Communicative skills before Reading/writing comprehension. Situational communication that is age-appropriate + applicable to the learners lives / specific needs. Applicable idioms/sayings. Comprehending/developing verbal language, appropriate intonation from peers as well as teacher.
⑤th	
How to know if SS are learning?	Via tasks + drills practicing target language usage AND allowing SS to conduct natural convos in class but facilitating convos to provide perfect opps for target language to be used. Gradually hearing less dependence on native lang AND/OR mixture of L1+L2. Taking notice if SS + T are able to understand what each other are trying to say.
⑥th *gradually relying less on gesturing + SS still understand*	

Relating to SS learning an L2 lang ⑦th	· Very useful + valuable · If T has/is also (been) L2 learner of some language. Can relate + adjust content accordingly due to similar experiences.
Methods/ approaches ↓ (1st topic addressed?)	· Communicative classrooms

Reflections teaching in MX

MAIN
POINTS
: o
: o

Reflection RD

Main themes:
- 1st time teaching
- 1st authoritative role involving multiple children
- how it affects future teaching method/approach
- sparked my interest

Stand out points:
- differences in learners (behavioral, age, interest, retention, exposure)
- o — importance of manipulating CR to keep children engaged
- ★ — SS very loving
- ★ — Need for praise + posi reinforcement
- o — more engaged, less problems (talk about implementing multiple activities w/ varying degrees of difficulty + diff materials)
- age-appropriate
- ★ — Relationship building

Key Experiences	Personal Responses	To Share
· Student engagement key to their success (classroom mngment too)	difficult to shake out achuities but themes/topics easy; some achuities differences, misbehave when bored	
SS very loving	motivational + inspiring to be better teacher, relationship building came naturally	
Spontaneity!!! diff's in learners (progress, exposure, interest, etc.)	acquired skill; hard to keep up. Changing LPs live in class. Changing activities mid-lesson. Getting to know SS easier w/ trgt + effort.	
Positive Reinforcement in classroom mngmt. benefitted as incentive / personal help	classroom mngmt more than PP; thus moving more often to LPs instead of CM. More focus. Nice seeing SS grow confident	
MRSA time exp. w/ this, but interactions	Reflecting back to personal exp. w/ L2 learning helped. I want to do this + progress	

Reflection Organization

Potential thesis (2nd):
- eye-opening
- 1st time
- Rewarding
- Inspiring / sparked interest
- Insight on how SS learn
- Interacting w/ children in an educational setting

Expectation (1st): Prior experience in tutoring pales in comparison to having own classroom. Expected to have purely communicational / discussion based classes that fit into a perfect TBLT bubble. W/ little attention / behavior issues + SS w/ more practice / exposure to English language.

Conclusions: (3RD)
[to share column]

Conclusion / Summary (4th): Overall, ~~~~ and I definitely want to progress.

See our range of fine, illustrated books, ebooks, notebooks and art calendars:
www.flametreepublishing.com

This is a **FLAME TREE NOTEBOOK**
Published and © copyright 2017 Flame Tree Publishing Ltd

FTNB 100 • 978-1-78664-000-0

Cover image based on a detail from
the Alhambra Palace
© liquid studios/Shutterstock.com

The Alhambra Palace in Andalusia, Spain, is a masterpiece of Islamic art. Each year, the World Heritage Site draws a staggering amount of visitors, who marvel at the richly ornamented architecture and its cultural significance. This beautiful tile work from the Mexuar in the Royal Palace demonstrates the intricate decorative patterns that can be found throughout the Alhambra.

FLAME TREE PUBLISHING | The Art of Fine Gifts
6 Melbray Mews, London SW6 3NS, United Kingdom

All rights reserved. Printed in China. Created in the UK.